BROWN BEAR WON'T TAKE OFF HIS COAT

Published in the United States by Debonæress™ an imprint of 31st & Seventh Publishing,
PO Box 290405, Port Orange, FL, 32127

Copyright © 2019 by Dr. Poochie

BROWN BEAR WON'T TAKE OFF HIS COAT/Dr. Poochie

Part One of the "Grow Together" series

Includes activities.   ISBN-13: 978-0-9904537-7-2

BROWN BEAR WON'T TAKE OFF HIS COAT

by Dr. Poochie

All Rights Reserved. No part of this publication, whether in print, audio or audiovisual, may be reproduced, stored in a retrieval system, or transmitted, in any form or by any means, whether electronic or mechanical, including photocopying, recording, or otherwise, without the prior written permission of the publisher.

Portions of the narrative in Part II attributable to findings as reported by Mark J. Biel and Kerry A. Gunther. March 2006. Information Paper No. BMO-10. Bear Management Office. Yellowstone National Park. https://www.nps.gov/yell/learn/nature/denning.htm

Special thanks to the experts at Achieve the Core. Hard Copy Printed in the United States of America

BROWN BEAR WON'T TAKE OFF HIS COAT

Features:
Picture cues/Visuals to support comprehension; Activities to promote memorization, fine motor skills, recall and critical thinking, Audio (optional), Video (optional), Vocabulary exposure, colors, high interest and motivational learning activities

Dr. Poochie

Author of Teaching High School: A Non-Fiction Horror

Mr. Melvin Marmoset

Mrs. Myrtle Marmoset

Olive the Orange Ostrich

Brown Bear

White Woodpecker

Red Rooster

Light Green Lizard

I invite Green Lizard

and White Woodpecker, too.

Myrtle Marmoset is ready for our guests to arrive. Napkins and bowls, no spoons or knives.

Come inside and take a look at all the good food Mrs. Marmoset cooked.

Fresh fruits and grains make a tasty dish.

And for Brown Bear, there's even a fish!

We hear a tap, tap, tap!
Someone's knocking at the door.

TAP!
TAP!
TAP!

Through the peephole, I could only see a great big smile.

Why, it's Olive the Orange Ostrich here to sit for awhile.

"Hello, Olive. What brings you here?" I asked filled with glee.

"Well," said Olive, "it's dinnertime. Do you have something for me?"

"Well, yes!" I replied. "The wife has prepared a special treat."

"Please come in, wipe your feet, watch your head and have a seat."

Olive the Orange Ostrich was careful to lower her head as she entered our small house.

She removed her yellow and blue hat from atop her head and handed it to me.

I hung it on the coat rack, careful as I could be.

"Oh Myrtle!" I called. Add a chair for Olive, please."

"Okay," she replied. "I'll gather pebbles and green leaves."

Just as Olive was sitting in her chair, there was another tap, tap, tap!

Maybe this time, it's Brown Bear.

When I peeped through the peephole,

I saw trees, nothing more.

When suddenly I spotted a white wing zooming past the door.

It was White Woodpecker!

She flew past me, whoosh!

Red Rooster wobbled in right behind her, giving my leg a push!

I laughed. "Well, well. Hello, both of you."
Woodpecker, may I take your scarf? And Red Rooster, your cane?"

"Thank you," they said in unison, scurrying in from the rain.

Our three guests began to chatter so loudly with Mrs. Marmoset that no one heard the next tap, tap, tap on the door.

Suddenly, a small voice was heard yelling, "Hellooo." "Helloooo!" Everyone turned toward the coat rack.

Mrs. Marmoset yelled, "Light Green Lizard, how did you get in here?"

Using his tail, Light Green Lizard pointed to a crack in the door.

"Come come, Lizard," I said. "Let me take your gloves."

"Thank you, Mr. Marmoset. The puddles outside have made it quite difficult for me."

"Ah," I replied. "Has the wet ground caused you to lose your grip again, old boy?"

"I'm afraid so. I'm happy to see that the sun is up and the ground and trees will be dry again soon."

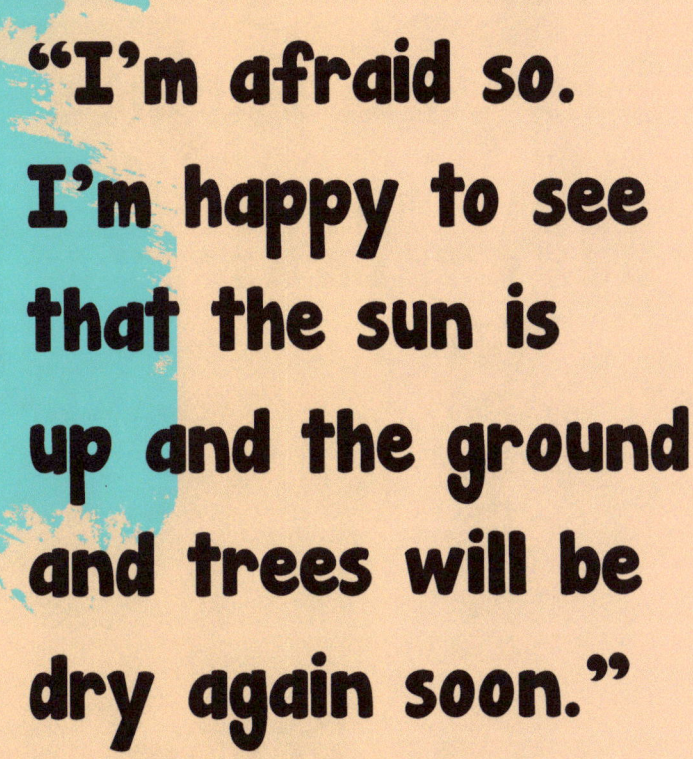

"Well, you are inside now, so feel free to run around to your heart's content. Just don't wander near the stew!"

Everyone laughed.

HA-HA!

HA-HA!

HA-HA!

HA-HA!

I added Light Green Lizard's gloves to the coat rack

.....and made room for him at the table.

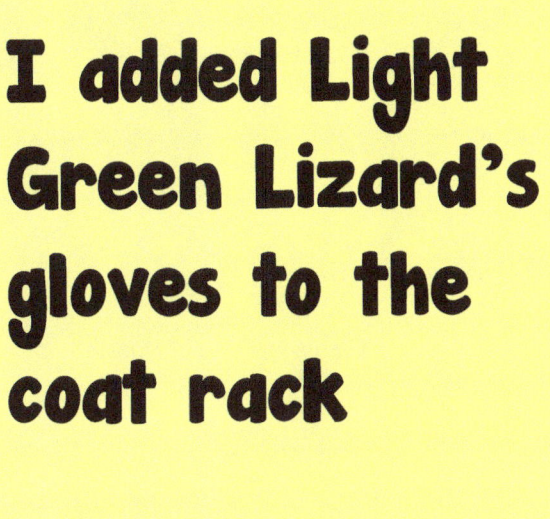

The next sound everyone heard was much louder than tap, tap, tap!

The Bang! Bang! Bang! was so loud, it rattled our old wooden house.

There was only one friend in all the forest who knocked on my door with such force. I began calling to Brown Bear.

"Is that you, my dear friend?"

"Yes, it is Brown Bear and I am very hungry!"

I opened the door. "Come in, Brown Bear. Come in, and...watch your head."

Brown Bear waved one of his big paws to everyone, as he looked for an empty seat at the table.

"Let me take your coat," I offered.

"Melvin, we've been through this. I would prefer keeping my coat on at dinner."

Myrtle and Melvin eyed each other. The room fell silent. White Woodpecker spoke up.

"Brown Bear, are we your friends?"

"Well sure you are."

"Then I think it is time for you to tell us."

"Yes," chimed in Olive the Orange Ostrich, "tell us why you won't take off your coat."

"Is it too heavy for the coat rack?" asked Red Rooster.

 "Will you be cold if you take it off?" asked Light Green Lizard.

"No, no," cried Brown Bear.

"Are you afraid you'll forget it when you leave?" asked Mrs. Marmoset.

"That's not it," retorted Brown Bear.

"Humph! You think I'm going to steal your furry coat, don't you?" teased White Woodpecker as she flew over to Brown Bear, perching herself on his left shoulder.

The others laughed. They knew Brown Bear trusted each of his friends.

But all their questions made poor Brown Bear so uncomfortable, he replied, "It's just that, well, I can't."

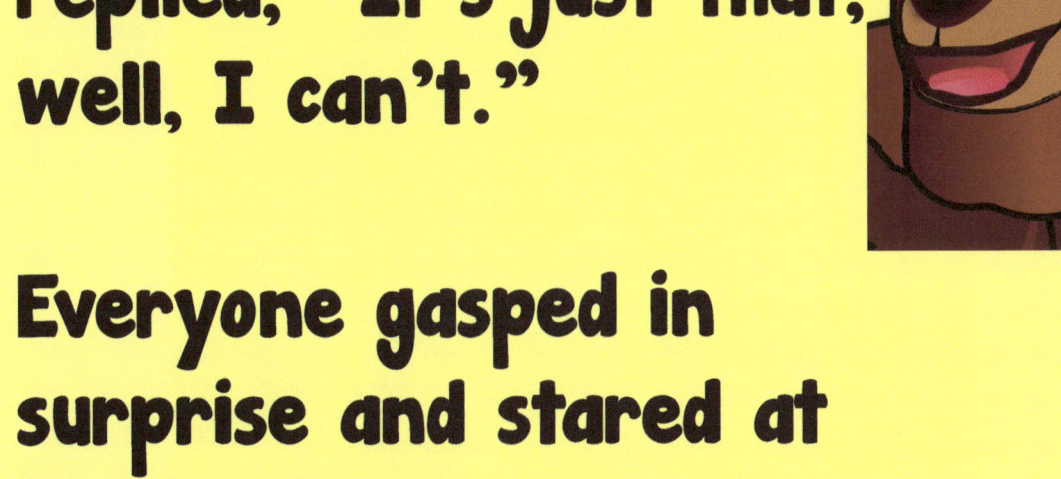

Everyone gasped in surprise and stared at Brown Bear. "You mean you're stuck in that coat forever?" cried Red Rooster.

"I mean, it's not as easy as taking off gloves or a scarf or shoes."

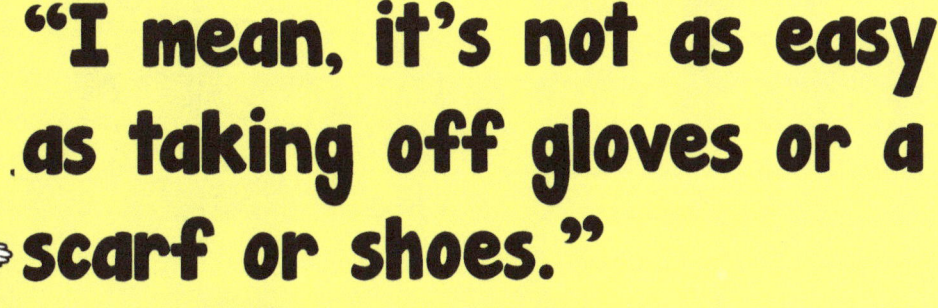

"Well tell us, Brown Bear. Our food is getting cold and I have a long journey ahead of me," bellowed Olive.

"Okay, okay!" Brown Bear stood up.

"You know how I told you I go away each year to visit my great aunt? "Yes."

"Of course."

"Sure."

"Uh huh."

"Well, I don't really go anywhere. I do this thing cal--"

"--what thing, Brown Bear?" Light Green Lizard interrupted.

"I uh,"

"Dinner's getting cold," chimed in Red Rooster.

"I hibernate. There, I said it."

"You hyper-what?" repeated White Woodpecker.

"Not hyper, hi-ber-nate. I hibernate."

"Is that against the law?" inquired Mrs. Marmoset.

"No, no. It's not against the law. I hibernate to survive the cold winter months.

"Well, once dinner is served, you can tell us all about it, er, while we eat."

Mr. Marmoset glanced at his wife. Mrs. Marmoset served the vegetable stew to all the dinner guests.

So, Brown Bear took a deep breath and began telling the story of hibernation.

The End

Draw a line from the Characters to their names:

Mr. Melvin Marmoset

Mrs. Myrtle Marmoset

Olive the Orange Ostrich

White Woodpecker

Red Rooster

Light Green Lizard

Brown Bear

Color the characters their correct colors.

47

Rhyme Time

Match the words that rhyme.
The first 2 have been done for you.
　　　Four rhymes with door.
　　　Dish rhymes with Fish.

Smile ____ more ____ awhile *push

Glee ____ whoosh! __*rain *bear

Treat ____ cane ____ *me *door

Me ____ 　　　　　　*be

Critical Thinking

1. In the story, do Brown Bear's friends seem happy or sad? Explain.

2. Why does Mr. Marmoset invite Brown Bear to his home to eat?

3. Brown Bear told his friends that he visited his great aunt every winter. Why did he tell them that? Was he telling the truth?

4. At the beginning of the story, Mr. Marmoset told us about all of his friends, except Olive the Orange Ostrich. Why didn't he mention Olive?

Memory Recall

What foods did Mrs. Marmoset prepare for her guests?

The first one is done for you.

Bananas

Comprehension

Olive the orange ostrich was the first guest to arrive. Was Mr. marmoset expecting her?

___

Why did he ask Olive to watch her head?

___

What did Olive eat for dinner?

___

What special food did Mr. Marmoset prepare for Brown Bear? (It rhymes with dish).

___

At the end of the story Brown Bear teaches his friends a new word what is it?

___

Match the <u>object</u> to its owner.

Match the <u>object</u> to its owner.

Cane

Scarf

Hat

Gloves

Purse

Color the Fish

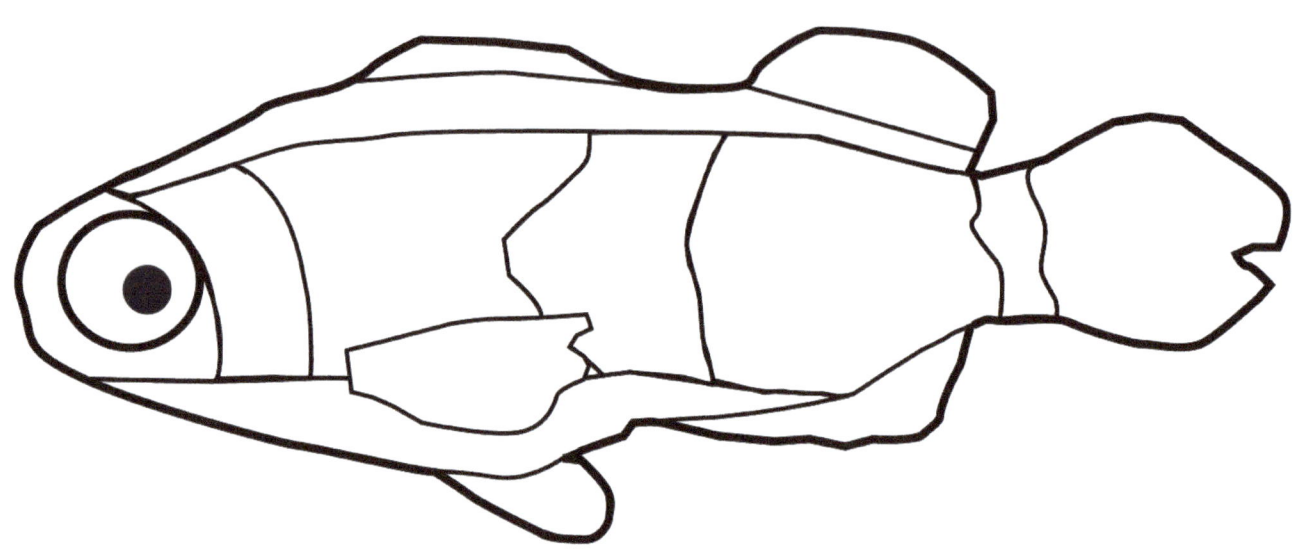

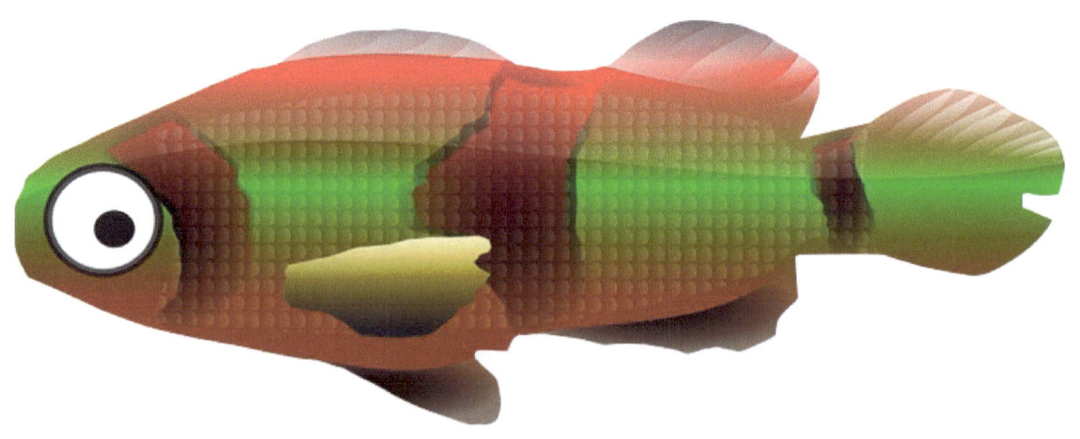

Phonics, Word Recognition, Fluency

A	B	C	D
afraid	breath	caused	deep
against		chimed	difficult
ahead		could	
asked			
atop			
away			

Phonics, Word Recognition, Fluency

E	F	G	H
eyed	force	gloves	heart
	forks	grains	heavy
	fruits	great	house
	furry	ground	
		guests	

Phonics, Word Recognition, Fluency

I
Interrupted

J
journey

K
knock
know

L
laughed

M

N

O
others

P
peeping
pointed
prefer
puddles

Phonics, Word Recognition, Fluency

Q	R	S	T
quite	rattled	scarf	through
		scurry	treat
		shoes	
		shoulder	
		special	
		spoke	
		surprise	
		survive	
		steal	
		still	

Phonics, Word Recognition, Fluency

U
Uncomfortable

V
vegetable

W
watch

X

Y

Z

Coming Soon, Part II

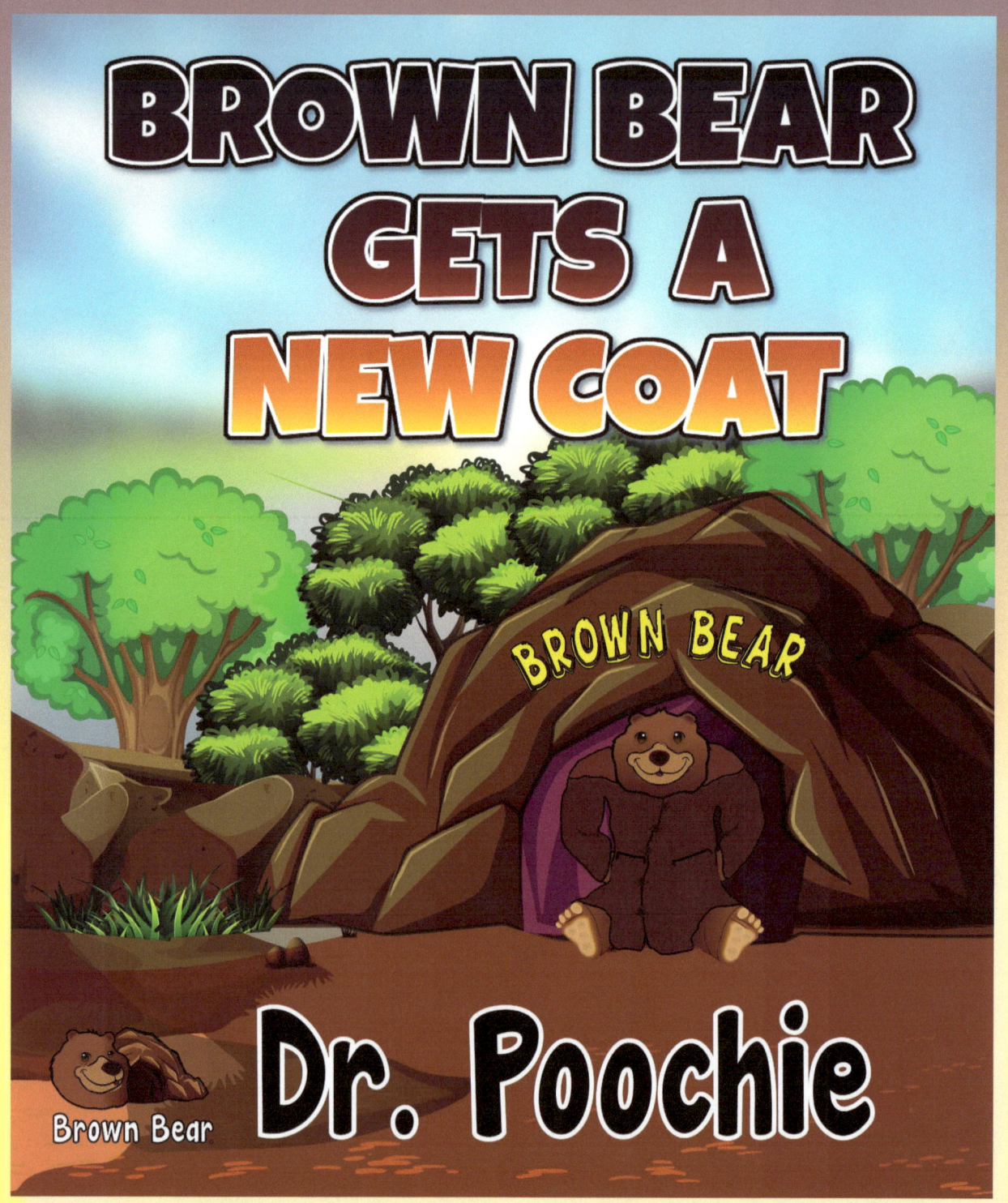

www.ingramcontent.com/pod-product-compliance
Lightning Source LLC
Chambersburg PA
CBHW041526220426
43670CB00002B/44